Original title:
Whispers of the Willow

Copyright © 2025 Creative Arts Management OÜ
All rights reserved.

Author: Jameson Hartfield
ISBN HARDBACK: 978-1-80566-626-4
ISBN PAPERBACK: 978-1-80566-911-1

## Songs of the Swaying Elders

In the park where the trees dance,
Elders leave their secret glance.
"Why do you sway?" I ask with glee,
"Because we're bored, just wait and see!"

Swaying left and then quite right,
They giggle in the pale moonlight.
"How's the weather in your leaves?"
"Dull as dirt, and full of thieves!"

Rustle, rustle, hear the cheer,
The squirrels gather, bring their beer.
"Let's toast to branches, wide and free!"
"And to those acorns, not for me!"

So if you wander, don't forget,
To chat with trees without regret.
They'll share their jokes, let's make them sing,
A dance beneath the boughs—oh, what a fling!

## The Language of the Swirling Leaves

Leaves are fluttering, having a ball,
"Do you hear the gossip?" one starts to call.
"Oh yes, I heard about the wind's affair,
He's blowing kisses everywhere!"

With a twirl, they spin in place,
"Did you see that squirrel? What a face!"
"He thinks he's cool with that nutty style,
But those acorns? Not worth his while!"

The branches shake with laughter bright,
Chirping birds join the silly fight.
"Let's start a chorus, loud and clear,
Winds of folly—let's all give a cheer!"

In the realm where all leaves converse,
They find fun in every universe.
So listen close to the rustling spree,
For the tales they tell are quite the spree!

## Conversations with the Timeless Sky

Oh sky above, with clouds so wide,
"What do you think?" the trees confide.
"I think you're looking quite a mess,
Your hair's a tangle, what a stress!"

"Don't lecture me on having style,
You just hang around and wait a while."
The sunset chuckles, paints a grin,
"Is that a laugh I hear? Let's begin!"

Stars peek out, with twinkles bright,
"Let's have a dance, sky and night!"
"I'll sway a little, you shine away,
Together we lighten up the day!"

So sky and trees, each cloud and breeze,
Share moments that put minds at ease.
In the dance of time, so bold and sly,
You'll find the laughter high in the sky!

## Tales Carried by the Evening Wind

The evening wind starts to weave tales,
Through leafy paths and playful gales.
"What's that? A secret?" I wish to know,
"Oh hush now, it's a breezy show!"

A squirrel scoffs, with nut in paw,
"Did you hear about that raccoon law?"
"He stole a bike, now rides at night,
With wheels that sparkle, what a sight!"

The trees all quiver, laughing hard,
"Maybe next, he'll steal a car!"
And as they chuckle, branches sway,
Tickling the stars at end of day.

So join the fun, let spirits lift,
With stories carried on wind's swift gift.
In every rustle, laughter blends,
With tales of joy that never ends!

## Beneath the Veil of Green

In the shade where shadows play,
Squirrels plot their daring sway,
Acorns drop in wild surprise,
As birds laugh with big, bright eyes.

A hedgehog dressed in tiny shoes,
Sells tickets for the forest blues,
While rabbits dance in top hats fine,
All under the twisty vine.

In the breeze, the giggles arise,
From the trees that wear disguise,
Each leaf a friend, each branch a joke,
The bark laughs loud—oh, what a poke!

The toad croaks tunes both sweet and weird,
While beetles tune their chords so cheered,
Nature's circus, a joyful scene,
Life's merry dance beneath the green.

## **Secrets of the Arcane Grove**

In the grove where shadows loom,
Rabbits brew a herbal plume,
Wands of carrot spark and glow,
With bubbles popping, cheeky show!

The owls wear glasses, wise and round,
Deciphering the jokes they've found,
While frogs recite their silly rhymes,
As crickets chirp in perfect times.

A gnome with glasses bids a cheer,
For each odd sprite that wanders near,
With mischief dancing on the breeze,
The trees chuckle at all with ease.

As moonlight spills a silver grin,
The laughter wraps us like a skin,
In this grove where joy's the quest,
The secrets shared, we feel so blessed.

## Breath of the Verdant Spirits

In green whispers, secrets fly,
Pixies trading jokes nearby,
With vines like arms that stretch and sway,
Encouraging fun in every way.

A squirrel juggles with delight,
While fireflies twinkle in the night,
With giggles echoing in the dark,
As owls provide the perfect spark.

Mushrooms dance in little shoes,
While snails slip by with rhymes to choose,
The breeze is filled with laughter bright,
As all the stars join in the light.

With every rustle, tales unfold,
Of playful spirits, brave and bold,
In this embrace, we find our place,
In nature's laughter, a warm embrace.

## The Language of Rustling Foliage

In the hush where leaves exchange,
Whimsical tales that feel so strange,
A ticklish breeze makes branches sway,
While creatures giggle their day away.

A bear in boots attempts to dance,
While turtles try to take a chance,
Squirrels skitter, round they twirl,
As ladybugs begin to whirl.

With every rustle, secrets tease,
Laughter spins among the trees,
The blooms are smirking, playfully bright,
As the sun winks goodbye to night.

Oh, what joy this forest brings,
In each whisper, the joy of springs,
With tongues made of rustling grace,
Every leaf a smiling face.

## Rustling Secrets Beneath the Boughs

Under the tree, a squirrel named Lou,
Wears tiny sunglasses, thinks he's so cool.
He chatters and dances, all wild and free,
Waving his paws like he's on TV.

A rabbit joins in, with a hop and a skip,
In search of a snack, he takes a bold trip.
He snatches a berry, makes a big fuss,
Then trips on a root, oh, what a big plus!

The birds tease the critters, chirping with glee,
"Don't mind us, we're busy, just wait and see!"
They giggle and flutter, pretending to fall,
As they swoop down low, giving everyone a call.

The breeze shakes the leaves, joining the fun,
"All this excitement? It's just begun!"
Each critter delights in the play of the day,
Beneath the old branches where laughter holds sway.

## Echoes of the Silent Grove

In the silent grove, a snail named Sue,
Moves at her pace, never in a rush, too.
She glances around with a twinkling eye,
"Are you all busy? I'm just passing by!"

A hedgehog named Fred, with spikes all aglow,
Laughs at the chase, "It's all very slow!"
He teases the breeze, as it whiskers him here,
"Oh, hurry up buddy, it's almost a year!"

A cricket is singing, his tune quite absurd,
"Why can't we dance? We've got it, good word!"
The fireflies twinkle, igniting the night,
As the critters assemble for their grand delight.

With giggles and chirps, the evening takes flight,
In this funny grove, everything feels right.
They share silly stories, each one quite grand,
In echoes of laughter, all just hand-in-hand.

## **Dreams Cradled in Leafy Embrace**

A raccoon named Ray, in dreams he would bake,
Cupcakes and cookies, oh, how they would shake!
With paws all covered in flour and goo,
He laughs with his friends, "Come try something new!"

An owl named Olive, wise beyond her years,
Winks at the chaos, stifling her cheers.
"Ray, let's not burn down the whole forest floor,
Just keep it to muffins, they're tasty for sure!"

A turtle strolls by, with snacks in her shell,
"Do you need frosting? I've a puddle, so swell!"
As they mix and they stir, with delight in the air,
"Who knew baking's fun? We might start a fair!"

In dreams they discover, beneath leaves that sway,
A world filled with laughter, in their funny way.
With each little blunder, it's full of good grace,
Together they thrive in this leafy embrace.

## Shadows of the Gentle Canopy

In the shade of the trees, where the shadows play,
A raccoon throws parties at close of the day.
He says, "Bring your snacks! And let's laugh, my friends!"
As the moonlight glimmers, the fun never ends.

A badger named Bill brings out party hats,
With ribbons and colors, a feast for the bats.
They dance on the grass, with sprigs in their toes,
As laughter erupts in a rhythm that flows.

"Who ordered the pizza?" a bird waddles near,
Singing sweet lyrics that make them all cheer.
A squirrel offers nuts with a mighty great toss,
"This bash is a blast! No one's the boss!"

In the shadows, it's bright under twinkling stars,
With friendships that flourish where laughter is ours.
They gather together, as night turns to day,
In a gentle embrace, they let laughter play.

## **Chronicles Written in Bark**

In the forest, trees gossip real low,
Telling tales of the sun and snow.
Squirrels wear glasses, oh what a sight,
Debating on acorn heights every night.

Rabbits wear shoes, they dance and spin,
Foxes play poker, and never lose their grin.
The owls keep score while the crickets sing,
This woodland circus sure is a thing!

## **Melodies Beneath the Arching Limbs**

Beneath the branches, a band unfolds,
Singing notes that are slightly bold.
A frog beats drums with a slick, wet thud,
While a raccoon croons, creating a flood.

The branches sway to a funky beat,
Even the ants shuffle their tiny feet.
Daisies are dancing in cheeky delight,
Embraced in a jig that lasts through the night.

## Soliloquies of the Nature's Sentinels

The old tree guards secrets, whispers quite high,
While the bushes mock passersby with a sigh.
A squirrel gives orders with a bossy stance,
Each nut in the plan, a culinary romance.

The brook giggles softly, it's tickled by stones,
It tells of the fish and their slippery moans.
Ladybugs hold court, with hats made of grass,
Telling stories of summer as they share a glass.

## **Breath of Green Canopies**

The leaves chuckle softly in the warm breeze,
Tickling the birds as they settle with ease.
A skunk in a tux, so dapper and neat,
Gives a nod to the world, declaring it sweet.

The sunbeams get lost in a game of tag,
While shadows play hide and seek, oh what a brag!
A whisper of wind, a quick playful tease,
Leaves them all laughing, as if they're at ease.

## Secret Seeds of the Verdant Heart

In a garden where laughter grows,
Beneath the sun's warm, cheeky glow.
Seeds of humor take their flight,
Sprouting giggles, pure delight.

Bumblebees in polka dots,
Dance in circles, what a plot!
Tulips tell the best of jokes,
While daisies share their sunny pokes.

Silly rabbits hop around,
Chasing shadows, lost but found.
Petunias giggle, petals shake,
In this fun-filled leafy lake.

A tiny gnome with a bright blue hat,
Trips on roots, falls down—how 'bout that?
With every tumble, laughter leads,
The secret's out, it's funny deeds!

## Whispers Suspended in Time

A clock that laughs under the moon,
Ticking jokes in a merry tune.
Time has quite the sense of spree,
Frolicking through eternity.

Old chairs squeak with tales of fun,
Where grandpas share their best puns run.
Dust bunnies join the comic chase,
Giggling through an empty space.

The sun keeps playing peek-a-boo,
While shadows join the mimic crew.
With every tick and every tock,
Laughter blooms around the clock.

Old stones chuckle in their prime,
As echoes bounce beyond all time.
Memories tease the roots that bind,
In funny flashes left behind.

## Dreams Linger Beneath the Old Tree

Beneath the branches, dreams dance free,
In a hammock, swaying with glee.
Squirrels chortle, sharing tales,
As laughter rides the playful gales.

Bark tickles the back of my head,
While mysteries twirl in each thread.
Napping frogs croak a lullaby,
While butterflies burst forth to fly.

Wishes tossed like leaves in a breeze,
Bring chuckles from the gossiping trees.
A wise old owl winks, what a sight,
In a world where play meets pure delight.

In twilight's glow, shadows play tricks,
While crickets orchestrate the mix.
Dancing dreams fade with the night,
But the laughter lingers, ever bright.

## The Soul of the Twilight Woods

In twilight's gleam, the trees do dance,
With branches waving, they take a chance.
A squirrel is spinning tales of old,
Of acorn treasures and nutty gold.

The owls do hoot with comical flair,
While fireflies gossip in the cool evening air.
A raccoon prances, thinking he's grand,
Dressed in his mask, the woodland band.

Beneath the moon, the shadows sway,
The forest chuckles, come what may.
Each critter joins the merry choir,
Making mischief, they'll never tire.

So when you wander where the wild things play,
Remember the antics that brighten your way.
For in these woods, silliness reigns,
And laughter echoes through leafy lanes.

## Fables at the Foot of the Elder Tree

At the base of the tree, old stories unfold,
Where bramble-bearers lounge, and secrets are told.
A badger's up to his usual tricks,
While the wise old owl just snickers, and stics.

The rabbits hop in a comical race,
With wobbly legs, they fall on their face.
The hedgehogs giggle at their own spines,
As they stumble through fables, drawn by the pines.

A turtle bursts forth, slow as a snail,
Claiming he's quick, but his jokes often fail.
The keen ears perk up, waiting for jest,
In the circle of laughter, they feel truly blessed.

At dusk, when the stories take flight once more,
The deer join in, but can't find the door.
So they tap dance home through the shimmering light,
Underneath the elder, where laughter ignites.

## Threads of Time in the Woodland Whisper

In the quiet glen, time prances and plays,
As creatures share jokes in bewildering ways.
A snail tells tales of a race with a hare,
While the hedgehogs shout, 'We can't go anywhere!'

The mushrooms giggle, sprouting in rows,
Spilling puns like rain, as the laughter flows.
A chipmunk declares he's the king of the hill,
While the squirrels plot a curious thrill.

The moon adds a wink, casting shadows around,
As the frogs croak out in a chorus profound.
Each whispering leaf has a punchline to give,
In the dance of the woods, oh, how they live!

So follow the path woven thick with delight,
Where every little creature grins in the night.
In the threads of the trees, let your spirits soar,
And join in the riddle, forevermore.

## A Cryptic Breath of Soft Green

In vibrant shades of emerald hue,
The forest schemes with its playful crew.
A fox with a wink plots a clever design,
Hiding behind bushes, sipping sweet brine.

The leaves rustle soft, sharing secrets of fun,
While the frogs leap high, soaking up sun.
A bashful young deer trips over her feet,
Sending acorns rolling — oh what a feat!

The winds carry jokes that tumble and twirl,
As chipmunks jest with their acorn pearl.
The pine trees chuckle with each gentle sway,
Lending their voices to this merry ballet.

So wander here, let your worries go free,
In the playful embrace of this green jubilee.
For in every rustle, and laughter you find,
The spirit of joy is beautifully blind.

## The Breath of Dappled Light

Beneath the trees, a dance they do,
With branches swaying, in the hue.
A squirrel slips, a twig does snap,
And starts a game of acorn clap.

Sunbeams play, like tiny sprites,
Tickling leaves in silly flights.
A laughter here, a chuckle there,
Nature's giggle fills the air.

Bumblebees buzz with giddy glee,
As blossoms dance on windy spree.
With pollen coats, they jig and prance,
In this wildflower, buzzing dance.

So watch your step, and do beware,
Of mischief waiting everywhere.
For in this grove of leafy cheer,
The jokes of nature are quite clear.

## Lullabies on the Breezy Path

Along the trail where breezes tease,
The daisies nod with playful ease.
A child trails laughter, running fast,
While butterflies flit, wings unsurpassed.

The grass tickles toes, a gentle nudge,
As ants perform their tiny grudge.
They lift their burdens, never tire,
While crickets tune the night's attire.

A bird calls out a silly rhyme,
And all the trees begin to chime.
Each leaf has secrets, a joke to share,
In the rustling whispers, beyond compare.

So if you wander, take a pause,
And listen close, for nature's laws.
In every sound, a jest will hide,
On breezy paths, enjoy the ride!

## Murmurs from the Ancient Roots

Down deep below where stories sleep,
The roots converse in whispers deep.
They joke about the leaves above,
And chuckle at the skies they love.

Old trunks lean close to share a tale,
Of critter pranks that never fail.
With peeking eyes, they catch the scene,
As rabbits hop in leafy green.

Their laughter echoes, a wooden sound,
As shadows stretch upon the ground.
Mice converge for a gossip spree,
Telling tales of their wild jubilee.

So don't forget this ancient crew,
In nature's fabric, a silly view.
For every root that twines and curls,
Holds giggles of forgotten worlds.

## Sighs of the Lonesome Stream

A stream flows past with a grumpy pout,
It splashes rocks, oh what a clout!
With bubbles popping like giggles bright,
It spills secrets in the moonlight.

Fish tease the water with a little splash,
In playful darts, they dart and dash.
While reeds hum tunes to the passing breeze,
And frogs join in with croaks and wheezes.

The stones sit stoic, grinning wide,
As waters rush, they take the ride.
Each ripple carries a jolly jest,
As nature chuckles, feeling blessed.

So if you find a lonesome stream,
Remember it's part of nature's dream.
For every sigh of water's glee,
Brings laughter through the tapestry.

## Hushed Conversations of the Season

The branches giggle in the breeze,
Squirrels chatter, doing as they please.
The acorns fall with a tiny plop,
Nature's jokes just never stop.

A rustling leaf tells quite the tale,
Of birds making gaffes while trying to sail.
The sunbathing frogs mock the snails,
With silly leaps and comical trails.

Even the breeze can barely contain,
Its laughter through the gentle rain.
The flowers dance in a joyous spree,
As if they too have caught the glee.

So come and laugh beneath the trees,
Where nature's pranks are just a breeze.
With every rustle and cheerful hue,
Life's grand comedy is shared by few.

## Underneath the Canopy's Embrace

A shady spot for a tea-time chat,
The ants parade; oh, what's up with that?
Bees buzz in circles, plotting their pranks,
While butterflies throw colorful pranks.

The branches sway, a playful tease,
As squirrels hide nuts just to appease.
Chirps echo loud; a feathered choir,
Serenading bugs that never tire.

Dandelions giggle as the wind sways,
Their wishes float off; in jest, they play.
With every rustle, a secret shared,
Beneath the boughs, laughter is aired.

Let's gather here, beneath leafy shade,
Where nature's giggles are ever displayed.
In every nook, the mirth won't cease,
A canopy woven with joyful peace.

## When the Light Dances on the Water

Sunlight winks upon the pond,
Frogs leap up with a mighty bond.
The ripples ripple back a glance,
As fish swim by in a quirky dance.

Ducklings paddle in parade style,
Quacking jokes that make us smile.
A dragonfly zooms with flair and speed,
Hovering over, it takes the lead.

A splash erupts with a fish's fluke,
While frogs engage in funny crook.
The lilies nod, joining in the fun,
As nature laughs beneath the sun.

So take a seat along the shore,
Where giggles abound forevermore.
In this water ballet of pure delight,
Laughter echoes from morning to night.

## Reveries of the Leafy Canopy

High above, the leaves conspire,
In a breeze that's cheeky and never tires.
An owl hoots with a wise old jest,
While critters below take a cheerful rest.

The shadows play tag in the golden rays,
As sunlight dances through leafy maze.
A wisecracking crow struts like a king,
Announcing his reign with a raucous swing.

Next, a branch creaks; a squirrel squeaks,
In this funny realm, it's laughter she speaks.
The fox rolls by with a clumsy grace,
Chasing his tail in a dizzying race.

Gather round in this leafy retreat,
Where every sound brings a whimsical beat.
With chuckles shared in the rustling breeze,
In the canopy's giggles, we find our ease.

## The Caress of a Hidden Breeze

A breeze tickles leaves with a shout,
It rustles the branches, no room for doubt.
A squirrel's tail waves in a flurry,
While birds gossip gossip, in quite a hurry.

The flowers nod, like they know a secret,
While beetles boogie, quite out of the bracket.
A butterfly flutters, performing a spin,
Laughing at shadows as they lose to the wind.

A frog joins in, with a leap and a plop,
He croaks out a tune, gives the giggles a hop.
The grass tickles toes, a quirky parade,
Nature's own stage with no need for aid.

So dance in this glade, let your worries drop,
For laughter and joy are the best ways to stop.
The breeze is a friend, playful and bold,
While mischief unfolds in stories untold.

## Serene Stories Woven in Green

In a patch of green, where the daisies bloom,
A worm claims his throne, in his earthbound room.
With a wink and a nod, he shows off his sway,
Who knew squirming could brighten the day?

The ants march in line, all armor and pride,
Holding a picnic, where crumbs reside.
A tiny parade, with cheese crumbs and cheer,
They hush each other, 'The queen will be here!'

A ladybug lands, her spots in a dance,
"Join my party!" she calls, with a flick and a glance.
The flowers respond, their petals all twirled,
Caterpillars giggle, "What antics unfurled!"

So come to this place, where the green tales are spun,
And share in the laughter, there's joy for everyone.
For in every corner, fun stories arise,
With a wink of the sun and a gleam in the eyes.

## Tales of the Growing Shadows

As daylight hurries to close its wide eye,
Shadows stretch long, like they're learning to fly.
A raccoon peeks out, with a glimmering gaze,
"Oh look! Another mystery, let's start a malaise!"

The moonlight chuckles, as it joins in the fun,
Telling old stories of shine and of run.
With each wink it gives, the shadows grow bold,
Finding new pranks in the stories retold.

A cat with a pounce, like a ninja in style,
Turns a simple shadow into a toe-curling smile.
While crickets compose their late-night encore,
With beats that make squirrels dance across the floor.

So treasure the night, where the shadows do sing,
With laughter and whimsy, oh what joy they bring!
In this dark-turning garden, surprises arise,
With tales of the moon and the fun in disguise.

## Melodies of the Swaying Branches

Branches sway gently, in a dance of delight,
Tickled by breezes, they twirl through the night.
A bird drops a beat, in a cheeky ballet,
While leaves chuckle softly, 'Let's join this array!'

The sun dips low, painting dreams in the air,
Old trees share secrets, some too wild to bear.
With every soft rustle, new tunes come to play,
As nature composes its whimsical day.

A bush joins the chorus, with buzzing bees' hum,
Finding the rhythm, they let out a drum.
The flowers lean close, to catch every sound,
While keeping their petals twirled round and round.

So sway with the branches, in a jesting spree,
Where laughter and music compose harmony.
In this garden of giggles, let the melodies roam,
For joy is a tune we all can call home.

## Echoing Dreams in a Woodland Nook

In a nook where squirrels dance,
Their acorns roll, a playful chance.
One falls down with a great big thud,
And all the birds just laugh and chud.

A deer prances with a silly hop,
Chasing after a butterfly flop.
It trips and tumbles, what a sight,
Got up quick, danced away from fright.

A fox tells tales to a listening stone,
About a mouse who dared to moan.
But that small fellow scored a snack,
By sneaking home and making track.

So join the fun, don't miss a beat,
Nature's antics can't be beat.
In the woods where laughter plays,
Every critter's having fun-filled days.

## A Tapestry of Secrets Below

In the soil, a rumor spins,
Of gophers plotting silly sins.
They dig and dive, and once in a while,
Pop up with a mischievous smile.

A rabbit races, hops, and leaps,
While dreaming of vast carrot heaps.
He trips on roots, takes quite a spill,
But grins wide, a daredevil thrill.

Mice have meetings in their dens,
With tales of cheese and feline ends.
Each vote is cast with tiny feet,
On how to sneak, oh, what a feat!

So down below where secrets lay,
The woodland crew enjoys their play.
If you listen close, there's no distress,
Just chuckles echoing through the mess.

## **Tender Tunes of the Leafy Canopy**

In the treetops, the birds compose,
A symphony of flutters, a joyful prose.
A crow croons off-key, oh such a noise,
But with each squawk, the trees rejoice!

A squirrel jives to the rhythm right,
While napping bunnies bask in sunlight.
They dream of snacks, so sweet and grand,
Not caring where they took their stand.

The bees hum tunes, all buzzing proud,
While butterflies dance through the leafy crowd.
Their colors twirl in a lively spree,
Creating a sight that's pure jubilee.

Each leaf sings tales of drizzles and dew,
While the wind adds a laugh, all shiny and new.
In this canopy, joy takes flight,
Nature's concert: a delightful sight!

## Whims of the Emerald Haven

In emerald realms where shadows play,
Frogs wear crowns in a regal display.
They hop and croak in fancy attire,
Thinking they're stars; they never tire.

A turtle slides with a grin so wide,
Dreaming of races—oh, what a pride!
He dashes slow but claims victory,
With every step, a joke in history.

In the thicket, a badger schemes,
With tales of treasures and wild dreams.
But tripping over his own two feet,
He's laughing hard, love's golden treat.

So wander through this playful scene,
Where every day, it's like a dream.
Emerald haven, come take a dive,
In laughter's arms, we all revive!

## Serenade of the Wandering Twigs

Twigs on the ground start to sing,
Their tiny voices make nature's ring,
They jive and twist in a silly dance,
As squirrels roll by in a trance.

A leaf joins in with a giggle and cheer,
Declaring it's happy for all to hear,
The branches sway with all of their might,
Making the bushes burst into light.

An acorn pops like a drum in the glen,
Challenging critters to join in again,
With every bounce there's laughter about,
As the forest joins in a chuckling shout.

Under the stars, the twigs take their flight,
They twirl and swirl till the morning light,
In the grand symphony of rustling glee,
Nature's jesters play endlessly free!

## Reflections in the Still Water

In the pond, a frog tries to croak,
But catches a fly, it's all just a joke,
The water chuckles as ripples arise,
A game of reflections unfolds in the skies.

A fish swims by, it blushes and grins,
Feeling the laughter, it flips and spins,
The dragonflies buzz with a wink and a swirl,
As the daisies giggle and bounce in a twirl.

The stillness breaks with a splash and a plop,
A turtle, you see, decided to drop,
It lands with a sound that's quite hard to ignore,
So the water bursts out in a giggly roar.

Laughter rings out from the shimmering hue,
As nature confesses its joys, bold and true,
The pond's little players, all lively and bright,
Celebrate the silliness deep into the night!

## The Dance of the Latticed Sunlight

Sunlight streams through the branches above,
Creating a jig that the leaves all love,
They shimmy and shake, they twist and they twirl,
In a festival of giggles, the shadows unfurl.

A beam hits a branch who takes a deep bow,
While a butterfly flutters, oh look at it now,
Dancing in patterns so light and so free,
It's a waltzing delight, come join in with me!

The boughs bend low, like they're trying to peek,
While the ants on the ground hold a conga critique,
Each flicker of light adds a bounce to the day,
In a world where the sunbeams just want to play.

From dawn until dusk, the frolic won't cease,
Nature's hilarity brings giggles and peace,
With every bright moment, the woodland holds tight,
To the dance of the rays till the fall of the night!

## **Whispered Legends of the Forest**

In the heart of the woods, a tale comes to life,
Of a raccoon who threw a grand banquet rife,
With berries and nuts, oh what a spread,
The critters all laughed at the mess that they fed!

A badger named Frank served cider with grace,
But spilled it all over the squirrel's fine lace,
The laughter erupted, a comedic scene,
As they shoved all the plunder in pockets unseen.

At dusk, they recounted their funniest hits,
The owl rolled his eyes at their clumsy bits,
While the fox shared the tale of a snail on a quest,
Who pondered all night on who'd eat him best.

So gather around for the stories to tell,
Of woodland adventures, oh aren't they just swell,
In the laughter of life, every creature can see,
That the best tales are funnier when shared with a tree!

## The Comfort of the Old Trees

Beneath the shade, I hear a sigh,
Old branches bend, they know the why.
Squirrels chatter, plotting their snack,
While roots play peek-a-boo in a stack.

Gnarled and wise, they've seen it all,
From picnics to a kid's wild ball.
A tree with glasses sees every trend,
And laughs at lovers who can't quite blend.

Bark that's rough but spirits bright,
For every laugh, there's a gentle bite.
With knots and grooves, their stories climb,
And every twist? A joke in rhyme.

So next you sit with shade abound,
Remember the wisdom that laughs around.
Old trees may sway, but they won't fall,
With humor strong, they embrace us all.

## **Emotions Entwined in the Twigs**

In tangled twigs, a secret fold,
Romance and jokes through bark unfold.
Two robins squabble, a comical fight,
As they bicker over the best nesting site.

Upon a limb, a snicker arrives,
Sharing the gossip of woodland lives.
The owl hoots loudly, with a wink and a grin,
While the wise old crows just shake their wings.

Beneath the leaves, a laughter stirs,
Ticklish breezes and playful whirs.
Heartstrings twine, in a feathered embrace,
While squirrels display their clumsy grace.

Joy in every rustle and rattle,
In the leafy lanes, there's no real battle.
Nature's jesters, in their leafy nest,
Entwine the day with humor, at best.

## The Memory of Ages in the Forest

Among the trunks, ancient tales reside,
Of woodland shenanigans, nothing to hide.
With roots deep in dirt, they plot and they scheme,
Old trees tell stories that make us all beam.

With branches that creak, and leaves that sway,
They've seen every creature that danced on display.
The rabbit who tripped, and the deer on the run,
All captured in laughter, bathed in sun.

A time capsule of giggles, each knot a delight,
Where laughter rings out, from morn until night.
With echoes of giggles in every breeze,
Nature's punchline hangs like the softest tease.

So when you wander these paths so grand,
Know each rustle's a joke, as nature has planned.
For every tale etched in bark might just be,
A humorous hint of the forest's decree.

## **Dreams Carried on the Wind**

The wind whispers softly through branches so thin,
Tickling the leaves as the stories begin.
A playful gust sends acorns in flight,
While dandelions giggle, all day, all night.

Breezes caper through the pea-green grass,
Chasing shadows as the moments amass.
Birds chirp in jest, with comical cheer,
For fluffy clouds wear their laughter sincere.

Feathers float wildly, a dance in the sky,
As dreams drift along, they wave goodbye.
Hilarity stirs in the rustling air,
Nature's way of saying, "Life's never a square!"

So follow the breeze with a heart so light,
In the laughter-filled lanes where dreams take flight.
For every gust carries a wish or a grin,
On this joyful journey, let the fun begin!

## The Sigh of Time in the Forest

In a forest where squirrels play,
Time sneezes leaves that float away.
Rabbits dance in silly shoes,
While owls hoot their best blues.

Trees gossip in rustling tones,
About the oddity of rolling stones.
A bear juggles honey pots,
As frogs jump in poetic knots.

Mice wear hats and sip on tea,
Chatting 'bout the latest spree.
The whispers tease the buzzing bees,
As branches sway in gentle ease.

So if you wander through the green,
Expect the quirks yet unseen.
For every giggle leaves its trace,
In this funny leafy place.

## **Embracing the Twilight's Secrets**

As twilight wraps the day in cheer,
Even shadows can crack a sneer.
Fireflies wear their party hats,
While crickets chirp in joyful spats.

The moon giggles at the sun's old tales,
As raccoons knock over garbage pails.
Each star twinkles in a playful race,
With comets tripping in their space.

A fox sings to the sleepy owl,
Who grumbles back with a sleepy growl.
While bats fly by with goofy style,
The night rolls on, it won't stay awhile.

Laughter echoes in the dusky light,
Crafting stories 'til the morning bright.
As darkness embraces hidden fun,
In this whimsical twilight run.

## Quiet Tales from the Earth's Heart

Deep in the soil, the worms do chat,
About their juicy meals — how about that?
With every wiggle, a secret shared,
Even the ants feel slightly scared.

Moles make hats from the leaves they find,
Claiming it's fashion, quite refined.
While beetles roll their tiny balls,
Their laughter echoes through the halls.

Earthworms giggle in their sandy beds,
Trading jokes, spinning tales like threads.
The roots of trees tap dance in delight,
Making the gophers squeak in fright.

Beneath our feet, the fun abounds,
In the quiet, laughter resounds.
So step with care, and you might hear,
The joyful tales the soil holds dear.

## Fragile Whispers in the Twilight

In twilight's glow, the fireflies laugh,
Drawing maps with their glowing half.
A hedgehog pens a book with quills,
While the breeze carries their giggling thrills.

The shadows play hide and seek with light,
While owls blink slowly, missing the sight.
Crickets wear their tiny shoes,
And dance on leaves, expressing their views.

The stars hum tunes above the snore,
As foxes trot on the forest floor.
With each rustle, the stories grow,
Fancy footwork in the twilight's show.

So come and join this silly spree,
Where nature's jesters roam so free.
In every rustle, every fun-filled twist,
Lies a world of laughter, hard to resist.

## The Stillness of an Enchanted Place

In a glade where leaves might chuckle,
A squirrel wears a tiny buckle.
He leaps and flits, a sprightly sprite,
Chasing dreams till the fall of night.

The mushrooms giggle with delight,
As crickets play their tunes at night.
A snail slides by, slick as a grin,
Who knew this world could be such fun?

Beneath a moon that winks and blinks,
A frog joins in, a jester in sync.
He croaks his jokes, a ribbiting sound,
While fireflies dance all around.

In this realm of quirky cheer,
Even shadows have a sense of jeer.
Laughter floats on the evening breeze,
As joy takes flight among the trees.

## Chants of Nature's Sacred Spaces

A chipmunk hops with a cheeky flair,
It hides its snacks without a care.
While wise old owls sip tea so slow,
Who will win, the nerve or the show?

The breeze carries tales from the ferns,
Of how the playful raccoon learns.
When masked bandits raid the feast,
The gnome just chuckles, to say the least.

Singing insects play a merry tune,
Under the gaze of a laughing moon.
Each note a tease, a playful jest,
Nature's choir simply knows best.

Among the roots, a tale unfolds,
Of daring squirrels, and braver molds.
In a world where laughter's embraced,
Life's serious moments are better chased.

## The Dance of Shadows at Dusk

Just when the sun starts to retreat,
Silly shadows skip on tiny feet.
They sway and twirl, with glee they prance,
A moonlit ballet, what a chance!

A shadow cat pounces with a roar,
Then cantors off to explore some more.
A playful ghost drifts in a rush,
While toads and frogs begin to hush.

Laughter echoes from trees with glee,
As owls spin tales of mischief and spree.
Each twist and turn a comic act,
Life's urgent moments, turned abstract.

Yet in darkness, the fun won't rest,
As mischief reigns with bug and jest.
In the night's grasp, fun takes its dance,
Under the stars, they shake and prance.

## Echoes of Old Souls Amid the Bark

Old folks say, 'What's with the trees?'
They giggle under rustling leaves.
With branches waving, tales take flight,
They whisper secrets through the night.

A wise old crow claims he can sing,
But all he does is flap and cling.
He croaks a tune, a silly show,
The squirrels roll their eyes, "Oh no!"

The owls drop puns to keep spirits high,
"Who needs sleep when you can fly?"
Each bark holds tales, both old and new,
In this comedy of life's bright view.

So gather round, let's share and laugh,
Nature's quirks, our comic path.
With echoes ringing through the dark,
Even the old trees share their spark.

## Reflections Beneath the Canopy

A leaf fell down, it twirled with glee,
Said, "Why not join, come dance with me?"
A squirrel nearby choked on his nut,
"I'm busy, you twig! I'm in a rut!"

The branches swing low, with secrets to share,
"Tiptoe softly, we don't want a scare!"
A bird chimed in, with a hiccuped tune,
"Can someone tell me, what's up with the moon?"

A chatty raccoon rolled by on his back,
"Where's the party? Do I have a snack?"
The shadows chuckled, old friends in the night,
"Let's throw a shindig, it'll be quite a sight!"

So beneath the leaves, laughter did swell,
In a nook of the woods, where stories compel.
The magic of nature, so zany and spry,
Kept the forest alive with each giggle and sigh.

## Songs of the Night-Blooming Flora

The petals opened wide with a yawn,
"What's that? Is it time for the dawn?"
A flower sang notes that tickled the breeze,
While a snail replied, "I'll be slow to please!"

One bloom declared, "Let's have some fun!"
"I'll wear a hat, you bring a pun!"
The daisies looked on, with petals aglow,
"We could host a party, but keep it on the low!"

A nightingale joined in, with flair in the air,
"Just give me some rhythm, I'll dance without care!"
The lilies all giggled, swaying with grace,
"Let's make this a night we can't outpace!"

And under the moon with laughter bestowed,
These flowers found joy on their glorious road.
With petals a-sway, and roots feeling spry,
They sang to the stars, their spirits so high.

## Conversations with the Gentle Night

Under the stars, there's a tap-tap-tap,
"Who's at the door? Is it a bat or a chap?"
A chipmunk peeked out, with a curious twitch,
"I'll open it wide – but only a smidge!"

The moon chuckled softly, "Hello, little guy!"
"What brings you out, floating 'cross the sky?"
"I'm here for a chat, let's share some cheer,"
Said the sly little fox, not showing his fear!"

So they gathered around, the critters a-din,
With stories and riddles, their laughter akin.
The owl hooted wise, "Don't let silence creep,
Share your funny tales, they'll help you leap!"

The night wore a smile, as giggles took flight,
In a patch full of joy beneath twinkling light.
Each critter's delight, an enchanting refrain,
In the soft glow of laughter, they felt no disdain.

## The Still Voice of the Ancient Wood

The trees stood tall with a creaky tone,
"Hey, listen here, or you're on your own!"
A rabbit perked up, with a hiccuping laugh,
"What's so important? Is it about my half?"

The bark chipped in, with a raspy grin,
"There's a rumor about a frog wanting in!"
"What frog?" yelled a beetle, who spun in a flash,
"I once had a friend who'd make quite a splash!"

"He sings like a star, all suave and so bright,
Can he teach us the moves for a disco tonight?"
The squirrels all squeaked, "Oh, what a delight!
Let's throw a rager and dance 'til the light!"

So the woods came alive, with humor and fun,
In a celebration where everyone won.
As leaves swayed together, in a jolly old wood,
They danced in communion, as nature once stood.

## Whispers of the Earth's Heartbeat

In the woods, the trees do joke,
With roots that dance, they never poke.
A squirrel passed by with a nut so grand,
He tripped on a twig, it fell from his hand.

The mushrooms giggle, all in a line,
While crickets sing their silly rhyme.
The breeze tickles grass, they laugh and sway,
Nature's comedy show, on a sunny day.

## The Enchanted Eaves of the Forest

A robin wore a funny hat,
Said, 'Where's the party? Who's bringing the mat?'
The fox played chess with a hapless hare,
As the trees gossiped, with gossip to share.

The sunlight peeked through leaves above,
While the ladybugs danced, two of them in love.
A bumblebee buzzed with a comical flair,
Claiming it's royalty, so light in the air.

## **Faint Murmurs Beneath the Stars**

At midnight, the owls held a debate,
Who's the wisest? They're never late!
A star sneezed loudly, 'Ah-choo!' it went,
The planets laughed, 'What a heavenly scent!'

Fireflies flickered like tiny lights,
Chasing each other in playful flights.
The moon chuckled, glowing so bright,
'What a crazy, lively night!'

## Swaying Tales in the Moonlight

The willows swayed with stories to tell,
Of a turtle who danced, man oh man, he fell!
A raccoon juggled acorns with glee,
While the critters cheered, 'Come dance with me!'

The nightingale sang a wobbly tune,
As mice formed a line, starting to croon.
With laughter and joy, the woods came alive,
'Tis the best place to truly thrive!"

## Mysteries Hidden in the Ferns

Beneath the ferns, where secrets hide,
A rabbit wears a fedora, quite dignified.
With a twitch and a hop, he seems to grin,
Flirting with the breeze, a mischievous sin.

The mushrooms hold meetings, quite absurd,
Arguing about dreams, in a whispering herd.
A squirrel takes notes, with a tiny pen,
Charting the chaos of his quirky friends.

The snails debate speed—who's the best?
While the lazy old turtle just takes a rest.
A secret society formed in the shade,
Where no one is swift, but fun's always made.

So tiptoe through ferns, and you might just find,
A party of giggles, where all are aligned.
Their world is a puzzle, both silly and grand,
A comical kingdom beneath nature's hand.

## The Soft Gaze of the Evening Light

As day dims down, the fireflies dance,
With glow-in-the-dark suits, ready to prance.
They plot to outshine the stars overhead,
In a race to the moon, they all want to spread.

The bushes chuckle at the sun's soft retreat,
As shadows grow longer, and make them complete.
A raccoon in glasses, a scholar he seems,
Reads books with his paws, fueled by wild dreams.

The owls all gossip with their wise little eyes,
Exchanging the juiciest nighttime surprise.
And a cat in a hat ponders life's curious fate,
While eating a snack that is far too late.

So embrace the dusk, with its playful light,
Where laughter is loud, and everything's bright.
In the calm of the evening, seek joy and delight,
For the world is a canvas, painted with bright.

## Beneath the Silken Cascade

A brook babbles softly, with secrets it keeps,
While fish throw a party, and gossip it leaps.
A frog in a tuxedo croaks out a tune,
That gets all the critters to sway with the moon.

The daisies, they giggle, with petal-like grace,
As they dance in the breeze, in their flowery space.
A butterfly winks, with a flick of its wing,
"Join in the fun!" it seems to sing.

The willows sway gently, with their arms open wide,
Offering shade where whimsical dreams bide.
And there by the bank sits a jolly old goat,
With a beard full of stories and a quirky note.

So come take a dip in this magical stream,
Where laughter is loud, and it's all but a dream.
Under silken cascades, make laughter your aim,
For life in the wild is a beautiful game.

## **Stories Dropped Like Raindrops**

As rain begins falling, it tickles the ground,
Each drop tells a tale, quite silly and round.
A ladybug laughs at her dance in the rain,
Waltzing with puddles, like a joyous refrain.

The trees shake their branches, a musical thrum,
While squirrels dart about, in their rain-booted fun.
They slip and they slide on the slick, shiny leaves,
Cheerful they giggle, with antics that weave.

A snail's race begins, oh what a delight,
As competitors cheer from the branches so tight.
Each droplet a thrill, each splash a big shout,
In this rain-soaked world, there's no room for doubt.

So dance in the downpour, let worry drift by,
For stories dropped like raindrops never say goodbye.
They shimmer in laughter, like pearls on the ground,
In the playful embrace of a friendship profound.

## The Hidden Lull of the Glade

In the quiet glade, critters play,
A squirrel races the leaves all day.
A frog croaks loudly, thinks he's a star,
While a shy mouse giggles, saying, "Ain't that bizarre!"

The breeze teases branches, a tickle on bark,
A dance of the shadows, a whimsical spark.
Robins tune up, a chorus so sweet,
As dragonflies zoom by, skipping a beat.

Under the sun, the grass grows tall,
A shy rabbit whispers, "I'll not take the fall!"
But a clumsy raccoon, with paws in a twist,
Stumbles on daisies, oh, what a list!

As day turns to dusk, they form a parade,
In critter confetti, all worries do fade.
With laughter and antics, they blend and unite,
In the hidden lull, everything feels right.

## Echoing Dreams in the Thicket

In the thicket where giggles collide,
A hedgehog spins tales with great pride.
Tales of his journeys, all wild and grand,
And a snail rolls his eyes, "This isn't quite planned!"

The owls make notes, a comedy show,
While the bunnies plot pranks down below.
A beaver dressed sharply in sticks and in leaves,
Says, "I build the best dam, just see what it achieves!"

Fireflies flicker a gentle light,
As crickets join in, a musical night.
Each note is a riddle, a joke in disguise,
Laughter erupts from the deep, starry skies.

So join the fun, let your spirit run free,
In the thicket of dreams, it's a raucous jubilee.
With echoes of giggles that float on the breeze,
You'll find magic here, among all the trees.

## **The Quietude of Embracing Branches**

Under the branches, secrets do lay,
As squirrels debate the best nut buffet.
A wise old owl, with spectacles round,
Nods at the chaos that's circling 'round.

The branches shake lightly, a tickle in air,
As a chipmunk, quite cheeky, swings without care.
With acorns as grenades, they create quite the scene,
Their laughter resounds in playful routine.

The shadows play tag with a soft, gentle sigh,
While the breeze lifts the leaves, oh my, oh my!
A pair of small robin, chirping a tune,
Keeps time with the rustle beneath the bright moon.

In the dance of the branches, a comfort we find,
With whispers of joy and a dash of the kind.
The night rolls on with each little shout,
In this quietude, all fun's about!

## Haven of the Fleeting Moments

In a haven so fine, where the butterflies meet,
A deer sneezes loudly, unsettling the beat.
The sunflowers giggle at a bee's awkward dive,
While a lizard looks on, feeling quite alive.

Moments of mischief float through the air,
As a rabbit's bright socks cause quite a scare.
"Those aren't very hide-y, my friend, can't you see?"
Chuckles an old tortoise, so wise and so free.

The shadows embrace, as the fireflies light,
Each flicker a memory, so genuine and bright.
With laughter all around, both wild and serene,
They bask in the joy of moments unseen.

So sift through the laughter, the cheer that it grants,
In this haven of moments, the heart simply chants.
With creatures and giggles drawing you near,
Every fleeting moment is savored with cheer.

## The Sway of an Unwritten Narrative

Once a tree had tales to tell,
With leaves that giggled, oh so well.
It swayed and danced in morning light,
Pretending to be quite the sight.

A squirrel passed, with acorn bold,
The tree exclaimed, "You're rather old!"
The squirrel grinned and tossed it high,
Saying, "At least I can still fly!"

A bird alighted on a branch,
To sing of dreams and take a chance.
"Your roots are deep but I am free!"
The tree replied, "You can't stump me!"

Around the trunk, the rabbits played,
In shadows where the sun had strayed.
They laughed at every twist and bend,
For nature keeps a silly trend.

## **In the Embrace of Fluttering Shadows**

Beneath the leaves, a shadow creeps,
Where little critters gather heaps.
A rabbit's wiggle, a fox's grin,
In this shady spot, it's where they win.

The owl hooted, with wisdom grand,
"You silly ones, don't understand."
The shadows danced, with frantic glee,
Their laughter echoed, wild and free.

A flicker here, a flutter there,
Bees buzzing on without a care.
They call out jokes that none can hear,
But every chuckle draws them near.

So in this glade of fun and cheer,
Each creature finds their place right here.
For even darkness has its flair,
In hidden whispers, full of air.

## **Gentle Murmurs Beneath the Boughs**

By the brook, a frog sits still,
With dreams of leaping, oh what a thrill!
He croaks out tales of sunlit days,
And giggles softly in his sway.

A snail nearby, with wisdom slow,
Says, "Take your time, don't rush the flow!"
The frog just laughs, then takes a hop,
While snails trip over, down they flop.

A family of birds with tunes so bright,
Decide to gossip from a height.
Their chatter fills the leafy space,
Join in the fun, just pick a place!

Underneath the boughs, laughter rings,
Nature knows how to play with things.
So frolic, jump, or simply chill,
Life's a comedy, if you will.

## Secrets of the Silent Grove

In the grove where secrets dwell,
A chatterbox of trees, they tell.
With branches shaking, leaves a-flutter,
They spill their tea, all warm and utter.

A hedgehog trotted, pricked with pride,
Eavesdropping on the gossip's tide.
He snorted loud, then snuck away,
"Some secrets are not mine to play!"

The wise old oak cracked up a joke,
"Why did the branch refuse to poke?"
The laughter spread from tree to vale,
As every leaf began to wail.

In this quiet, silly place,
Every creature finds some space.
For in the silence, joy does bloom,
Even the shadows find their room.

## **Soft Echoes unto the Meadow**

In the meadow where grasses giggle,
A cow sneezed loud, and made a wiggle.
The flowers danced, they laughed so sweet,
As the sun tickled their tiny feet.

Bunnies hopping in a parade,
Each with a hat that they had made.
They twirled and spun on a dandy spree,
Chasing shadows from a bumblebee.

Clouds above threw a fluffy joke,
As rabbits wore glasses, a silly poke.
With tiny umbrellas for the breeze,
They splashed in puddles, oh what a tease!

Amidst the fun, a squirrel marched through,
Fashioned a cape of leaves and glue.
The creatures cheered, all filled with cheer,
For the meadow's laughter was loud and clear.

## The Heartbeat of the Verdant Realm

In the woods where the critters plot,
Chirpy birds sing, all laughing a lot.
A hedgehog danced in a mismatched sock,
While turtles played tag, oh what a shock!

The trees would sway, a leafy groove,
As ants wore shades and began to move.
With tiny ties and briefcase in hand,
They hustled about, a busy band.

A frog on a lily pad took a caper,
Shouting, "I'm a prince! Just need a taper!"
The bugs rolled their eyes, they've seen this act,
"Come take a seat, this is quite the fact!"

Dancing fireflies lit up the night,
A party for all, what a delight!
In this realm where surprises seem real,
Every heartbeat adds to the appeal.

## Tranquility in the Folding Leaves

Leaves rustle with a cheeky tune,
As squirrels juggle nuts by the moon.
They tumble and roll, a chaotic scene,
The funniest show you've ever seen!

A wise old owl gave a quirky wink,
To raccoons who paused for a quick drink.
With hats made of acorns, they toast to the night,
As the stars join in, oh what a sight!

The breeze giggles, carrying tales,
Of a snail race with tiny sails.
"Let's make a bet," the critters decree,
"Who'll reach the end? It's anyone's spree!"

Under the canopy, antics unfold,
Nature's great stage, a comedy gold.
Where tranquility meets laughter in leaves,
The forest buzzes, no one deceives.

# Fables of the Glistening Dew

Dewdrops form tales on the grass at dawn,
A ladybug's laugh, a cheerful yawn.
While daisies gossip about the ants,
All with a twinkle, in morning pants.

A butterfly flutters in rainbow styles,
Complimenting beetles, all in smiles.
"Your shell's a treasure!" one bug does cheer,
As they dance and prance, drawing all near.

Bees buzz around with a hip-hop flair,
Singing of nectar, sweet beyond compare.
With tiny bling and a bee-dance move,
They show off their skills, oh how they groove!

The sun peeks in, with a playful grin,
Witnessing nature's cheeky din.
In this realm, where laughter's the cue,
The dew tells fables, bright and new.

## The Breeze's Quiet Confessions

The breeze giggles, skips around,
Telling secrets without a sound.
It tickles the flowers, makes them sway,
As they blush in a sunlit play.

A squirrel laughs, with nuts in tow,
Chasing shadows, putting on a show.
He trips on roots, sends acorns high,
While the wind just chuckles, oh my, oh my!

A bird soars past with a cheeky smirk,
Dancing on air, doing its work.
It chatters to clouds, so fluffy and white,
While the sun beams down, shining so bright.

So next time you hear the gentle breeze,
Know it's cracking jokes among the trees.
For nature's comedy is alive and well,
In whispers and rustles, it has tales to tell.

## Soft Shadows in the Dusk

as the sun dips low, the shadows play,
they stretch and yawn at the end of day.
a rabbit hops, in slippers so sly,
while a chirping cricket sings lullabies.

The dusk giggles, as creatures appear,
a raccoon prances, oh dear, oh dear!
it tips its hat, oh such a delight,
under the twinkling stars shining bright.

The trees high-five with their leafy hands,
spreading gossipy tales across the lands.
A fox rolls over, chasing its tail,
while the moon winks, in this cheerful tale.

In the soft embrace of twilight's glow,
the giggles of nature begin to flow.
it's a funny dance of shadows and light,
that warms the heart, as day turns to night.

## Lullabies of the Ancient Trees

Old trees whisper, with creaks and groans,
telling tales of mischievous gnomes.
they sway with laughter in the breeze,
sharing secrets, as sweet as these.

A cat climbs high, in a clumsy blend,
does a backflip, oh what a trend!
it lands with a thud, then shakes its head,
while the oak just chuckles, with leaves widespread.

The roots tickle bugs, as they scurry by,
a chorus of laughter, oh me, oh my!
the trees wear crowns, made of leafy green,
while squirrels audition for the grandest scene.

So listen close, to the ancient sounds,
of nature's humor, where joy abounds.
In every rustle, a giggle you'll catch,
like a punchline delivered with a perfect match.

## Echoes Among the Leaves

In the forest, a sound takes flight,
Leaves giggle softly in the fading light.
A raccoon trips, and what a sight,
As echoes ripple, in pure delight.

The branches sway, each movement a tease,
As squirrels plot their nutty expertise.
"Catch me if you can!" they leap and dash,
While the wise old owl just hoots and laughs.

A breeze helps the flowers to twirl and glide,
They dance together, with petals wide.
The sun grins down, a shining star,
As laughter spreads, near and far.

So stroll through the woods, with a smile in tow,
For echoes of laughter are sure to flow.
In nature's theater, the comedy thrives,
Where joy abounds and happiness thrives.

www.ingramcontent.com/pod-product-compliance
Lightning Source LLC
Chambersburg PA
CBHW071830160426
43209CB00003B/265